THE INHERENT GENIUS OF
SYLVESTER STALLONE

Hollywood's Most Under Appreciated Writer

By
TRAVIS CODY

Travis Cody

Visit the Official Travis Cody Website at:

www.TravisCody.com

Printed in the United States of America

First Printing: June 2017

Axios Publishing

ISBN: 978-1-545-41106-3

100% of the profits from this book are donated to Hire Heroes USA
www.HireHeroesUSA.org

Contents

The Hero's Journey 1

Introduction 3

CHAPTER ONE: A Little Context for Our Story. 7

CHAPTER TWO: The Memo That Started It All 11

CHAPTER FOUR: The Separation 13

CHAPTER FOUR: The Descent 23

CHAPTER FIVE: The Initiation 29

CHAPTER SIX: The Return 33

CHAPTER SEVEN: John Rambo - The 30 Year Journey 39

Epilogue 53

Works Cited 55

THE HERO'S JOURNEY

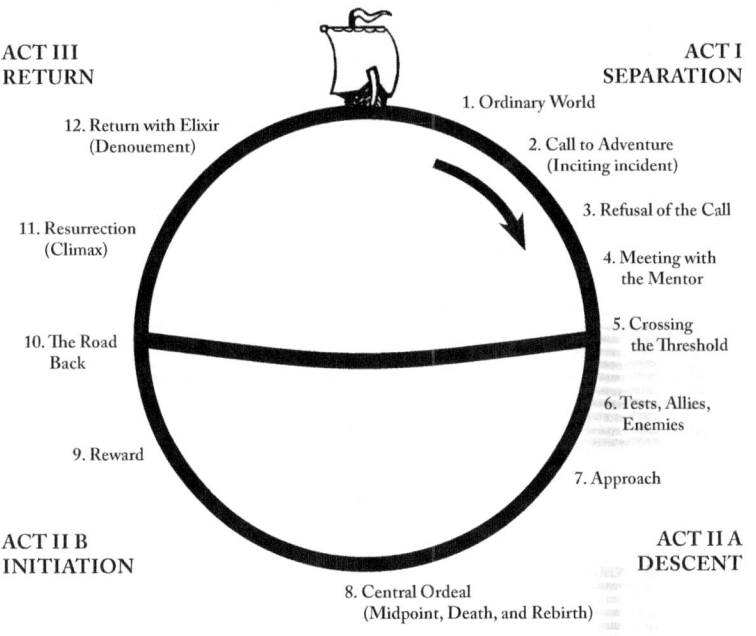

ACT III
RETURN

12. Return with Elixir
(Denouement)

11. Resurrection
(Climax)

10. The Road
Back

9. Reward

ACT II B
INITIATION

ACT I
SEPARATION

1. Ordinary World

2. Call to Adventure
(Inciting incident)

3. Refusal of the Call

4. Meeting with
the Mentor

5. Crossing
the Threshold

6. Tests, Allies,
Enemies

7. Approach

ACT II A
DESCENT

8. Central Ordeal
(Midpoint, Death, and Rebirth)

"A hero ventures forth from the world of common day into a region of supernatural wonder: fabulous forces are there encountered and a decisive victory is won: the hero comes back from this mysterious adventure with the power to bestow boons on his fellow man."

Joseph Campbell

1

Introduction

When the name Sylvester Stallone comes up, the first word association is: *Rocky*. Followed in quick succession by *Rambo* and *Action Star*. Rarely is the word "writer" ever mentioned. It's almost as if Stallone's shredded physique and the muscle head heroes that he's made a career from, have blinded people to a tremendously startling fact: Out of the 46 films that Stallone has starred in, 24 have been written by him! This is something that no other A-List actor can claim.

Also forgotten is the fact that in 1977 Stallone became only the third person in history to be nominated for an Academy Award for both acting AND *writing!* (The other two being Charlie Chaplin and Orson Welles). Unlike other, more recent, actors who make claim to have written their way to stardom... Stallone has *continued* to write one blockbuster film after another for over 40 years. And he shows no signs of slowing down. The Expendables (2010) opened at number one at the U.S. box office with a first weekend gross of $35 million. This makes Sylvester Stallone the only person in Hollywood history to have starred in films that have opened atop the box office charts over five consecutive decades.

As the former head of film development for producer Jonathan Krane, I've spent nearly 15 years tearing stories, ideas and scripts into pieces in order to analyze what separates the GREAT from mediocre or lame. One of the great privileges of working with dozens of massively talented writers has been to watch the creative process unfold and blossom.

At the core, has always been an underlying faith and belief in Joseph Campbell's "Hero's Journey." It's the one thread seemingly to tie all great stories together. While it's dangerous to suggest that there is a "formula" for writing a great film, since talentless executives and writers can suddenly proclaim that screenwriting is nothing more than a "paint by numbers" process, the Hero's Journey certainly offers a proven structure to emotionally moving stories.

As I've studied Campbell's works in an effort to uncover his secrets, as it were, a baffling fact popped up: most of what has been written about the Hero's Journey in Hollywood has been around a *single* film.

Stallone, on the other hand, has managed to do something that no other screenwriter in history has managed to achieve: A complete, faithful adherence to the structure not only just on the micro level of each film; he's also managed to do so on a macro level in which *each* film is its own separate piece of Campbell's 4-Step Circle. Even more incredible is when you consider the character with whom he accomplished this with: *Rambo.*

And therein lies the basis for this book. Sylvester Stallone, as a writer, has flown quietly under the radar for most people. It's a combination of his volume of work, along with the fact that it's been so subtle, that makes his accomplishments genius. And certainly makes him one of the most underappreciated writers in Hollywood today.

The short book you are about read was originally researched and written as part of my final Master's Thesis making it, at the time of this writing, the only academic work to be written around the writing of Sylvester Stallone and, more specifically, what he managed to achieve with his Rambo film series. I hope you enjoy it.

CHAPTER ONE

A Little Context for Our Story

The life's of work of Joseph Campbell has deeply impacted the entertainment industry, especially when it comes to movies. In Hollywood his theories, particularly those found in *The Hero with a Thousand Faces* and *The Power of Myth*, have become essential guides to anyone wishing to create a powerful, lasting story. "All stories consist of a few common structural elements found universally in myths, fairy tales, dreams and movies. They are known collectively as **The Hero's Journey**." (Vogler, xxvii) Some of the greatest and most financially profitable films of all time including *Star Wars, Titanic, Lion King,* and *Back to the Future* successfully incorporate elements of The Hero's Journey.

Few films, however, give as detailed a view of the journey on a micro and macro level as do the Rambo films written by Sylvester Stallone. These films epitomize the four primary stages of the journey which are Separation, Descent, Initiation, and Return. The character of John Rambo goes through all four stages during each film. Collectively, the four films also comprise the entire journey, with each film representing one of those arcs. The films provide a rare example of a Hero's Journey that takes over thirty years to fully complete.

In order to conduct a thorough analysis of the Rambo films the history and background of the Hero's Journey needs exploration first. Realization of the *content* of the films only happens with full understanding of *context*. What is the Hero's Journey? Where did it come from? How did it become the standard by which many Hollywood producers and studio executives now use to evaluate, analyze and create the films that they do?

Joseph Campbell graduated from Colombia University with a degree in English and medieval literature. Fascinated with the Native American artifacts he witnessed as a child, Campbell "became an author of comparative mythology. His work examined the functions of myth in cultures across the world and mythic figures in a wide range of literature." (Biography) While teaching at Sarah Lawrence College he attended lectures by prominent Indologist Heinrich Zimmer. When Zimmer died shortly after, Campbell undertook the task to transcribe his unpublished notes. The process took over twelve years and resulted in four books: *"Myths and Symbols in Indian Art and Civilization* (1946), *The King and the Corpse* (1948), *Philosophies of India,* (1951), and *The Art of Indian Asia* (1955)"* (Ibid). During the transcription Campbell was also writing his own book on myth titled *"The Hero of a Thousand Faces,"* which remains his best-known work. In it "Campbell tied the meaning of myth to its plot and claimed to have deciphered the common plot of all hero myths. He understood the hero myth's central plot in Jungian terms, defining it as the male or female hero's journey to a strange, new, divine world" (Ibid). In the mid-80's "Campbell's ideas exploded into a wider sphere of awareness with the Bill Moyers interview show on PBS, *The Power of Myth.*"

The show was a hit, cutting across lines of age, politics and religion to speak directly to people's spirits. The book version, a transcript of the interview, was on the *New York Times* bestseller list for over a year" (Vogler, xxxi).

CHAPTER TWO

The Memo That Started It All

A young Hollywood writer, Christopher Vogler, began to explore "Campbell's ideas of the Hero's Journey to understand the phenomenal repeat business of movies such as *Star Wars* and *Close Encounters*" (Vogler, xxvii). After going to work as a story analyst for the Walt Disney Company, Vogler "wrote a seven-page memo called 'A Practical Guide to *The Hero with a Thousand Faces*'" in which he "described the idea of the Hero's Journey, with examples of classic and current movies" (Ibid). "The Practical Guide" and Campbell's ideas began to have an effect on Hollywood. Vogler discovered "that executives of other studios were giving the pamphlet to writers, directors, and producers as guides to universal, commercial story patterns. Apparently, Hollywood was finding the Hero's Journey useful" (Vogler, xxx).

That seven-page pamphlet would eventually become a book over 400 pages in length (*The Writers Journey*) and spawn an entire industry that catered to writers and the Hero's Journey. Workshops, books, videos and elaborate computer software designed to trace every step of the journey sprang forth. Hollywood had begun its own journey towards deeper, more meaningful stories. During the same time that *Star Wars* and Close *Encounters of the Third Kind* were making history at the box office, a new type of hero quietly developed in the film *First Blood*, based on the book of the same name by David Morrell.

CHAPTER THREE

The Separation

"The Hero's Journey" starts when the hero leaves what Campbell refers to as the "ordinary world" and is called or forced into a "special world", or an environment vastly different than the one they start out in. This separation occurs during Act One of a screenplay. In *First Blood,* John Rambo makes his entrance as a drifter already separated from the ordinary world. Dressed in army fatigues with an American flag patch on the shoulder, he hikes to an isolated house looking for a friend from his days in Vietnam. When he discovers his friend dead, he moves on in sadness.

The Separation comes about from a call to adventure. "…The merest chance – reveals an unsuspected world, and the individual is drawn into a relationship with forces not rightly stood." (Campbell, 51) The local Sherriff stops Rambo as he approaches the nearest town and insists on giving Rambo a ride. During the ride, Rambo meets a force that will not be "rightly understood." As they drive, the Sherriff's line of questioning sets the stage for the events about to come.

TEASLE

Someone give you a ride into town?

RAMBO

No. Is there someplace I could get something to eat?

TEASLE

Sorry, we don't have Salvation Army soup kitchen in town.

RAMBO

I'm not looking for a handout.

TEASLE

Good. Then you'll find a diner about 30 miles up the road.

RAMBO

Is there a law about getting something here?

TEASLE

Yeah, me! (Stallone/Giler, First Blood, 10A)

Teasle makes it known immediately that *he* is the law around here and that Rambo's presence will disrupt things. "I don't want a guy like you around. Next thing you know, a bunch of your friends turn up. Besides, you wouldn't like it here. It's boring, but it's the way we like it. It's the way we like to keep it" (Stallone/ Giler, *First* Blood, 11). Teasle drops him off past the far edge of town. At this point Rambo confronts his first call to adventure: move on peacefully, or face Teasle's wrath. As Teasle turns around, he sees Rambo walking back towards town. Rambo has accepted the call to adventure.

Teasle arrests Rambo and hauls him to jail. While there, the deputies beat and abuse Rambo, which triggers his past trauma from Vietnam. When the deputies push Rambo to the breaking point, he snaps and escapes from the jail, seriously injuring the deputies as he does so. Leaving town for the wilderness fully cements Rambo's separation, as he has left the ordinary world of town for the dangerous cold of nature.

The second film, *First Blood: Part 2*, written by Sylvester Stallone and James Cameron condenses the first part of the journey – Separation and the Call to Adventure (the beginning of Act 2) – down to the first two pages. The story begins with Rambo in prison (the Ordinary World). Col. Trautman – fulfilling the role Campbell calls "The Mentor" – appears and offers Rambo a chance to get out of prison, plus a possible pardon, by helping with a special mission back to Vietnam. The "refusal of the call" happens in Rambo's reluctance to answer, as well as his admission that prison has become the Ordinary World for him.

TRAUTMAN

Johnny... I told you I'd help you when I could... you interested?

Rambo looks off at the distance, watching the Guards hang around off to the side.

TRAUTMAN (Continuing, taken aback)

You can't possibly want to stay in prison for another five years?

RAMBO

... In here I know where I stand. (Stallone/ Cameron, 2)

Rambo has become so detached from society, that prison, a "special world" to regular society, has become the comfortable ordinary for him. There are rules and ways of behavior that make sense. Trautman, being a wise mentor, explains that the mission involves P.O.W's and a return to a prison camp that Rambo had escaped from. When Rambo asks "Do we get to win this time," there is the sense that Rambo feels there were others who prevented him from winning before. Trautman answers "This time, it's up to you." Rambo accepts and the journey begins.

Rambo III starts much the same way as number two, only now Rambo lives in Asia working at a monastery. The Mentor again returns when Trautman finds Rambo and asks for his help with another dangerous mission. As with the majority of the stories that follow the Hero's Journey, the hero can accept or refuse the "call to adventure." "I've done my time," Rambo says and Trautman leaves. Rambo has had enough of the hero's journey. At the monastery he has found a place to call his own Ordinary World.

Stallone (and his writing partner Sheldon Lettich) twist the convention of the journey by allowing the Mentors downfall. When Trautman moves ahead on his own, enemy troops capture him. In most journeys, The Mentor serves as a sort of "supernatural aid" to the hero. "For those who have not refused the call, the first encounter of the hero-journey is with a protective figure (often a little…old man) who provides the adventurer with amulets against the forces he is about to pass" (Campbell, 69). In this instant, the Mentors capture *is* the call to adventure that the hero can't refuse.

Rambo, the fourth film in the adventure, occurs twenty years after the third. Rambo appears much older and more grizzled with the "separation" from the ordinary world of America having taken its toll. The "call to adventure" and Separation from his current Ordinary World comes when a group of missionaries solicits his help in traveling up river. After an initial refusal and strong word of caution that they abandon their quest, one of the group's members, Sarah, convinces him otherwise. She reminds Rambo that he too once stood for something.

SARAH

You don't agree with what we're doing, do you?

RAMBO

Doesn't matter what I think.

SARAH

I just wondered why you agreed.

RAMBO

You stand for something.

SARAH

So maybe you do agree with something we're doing.

RAMBO

...Maybe. (Stallone, 21)

In this moment Rambo also reveals the burden that has weighed him down and has prevented him from being able to America.

SARAH

Even though we can't do much more than bring medicine and some encouragement, we believe it will all work out in the end. Peace will come if you work at it.

RAMBO

You put out one fire, another starts.

SARAH

No, everything comes to an end.

RAMBO

Turnin' the other cheek doesn't work here. When something you love has been killed, there's no mercy, there's never enough revenge, even if you kill the enemy over and over, it's never enough – (taps his chest) *The war in here never ends* (Stallone, 22 – emphasis added).

A few days after he takes them up river they are captured. In previous stories, Rambo had a clear path and enemy. In this story, when Rambo reaches the First Threshold, he discovers that the thing preventing him from moving forward is himself. "The hero goes forward in his adventure until he comes to the "threshold guardian" at the entrance to the zone of magnified power. Such custodians bound the world in four directions – also up and down – standing for the limits of the hero's present sphere or life horizon. Beyond them is darkness, the unknown and danger…" (Campbell, 77).

Rambo didn't want to get involved. Not in Vietnam. Not in Hope (the town in *First Blood)*. Not in Afghanistan. He has spent his whole life trying to avoid his past. Indecisive on how to proceed, Rambo receives some "supernatural aid" in a visit by his Mentor via a dream. When Rambo dreams of the adventures of all his journeys thus far, Trautman appears and cautions him that he needs to let go of the past. That he won't be able to move forward and let go unless he comes "full circle." This supernatural visit allows Rambo to break through his threshold by accepting responsibility for his past. He was the one who created his life and events. With this realization also comes a resolve that Rambo hasn't had for a long time.

CHAPTER FOUR

The Descent

Once separated, the journey continues into The Descent, which correlates with the first half of Act Two in a screenplay. The hero "must survive a succession of trials. It's a new and sometimes frightening experience for the hero. We seekers are in shock – this new world is so different from the home we're always known. Not only are the terrain and the local residents different, the rules of this place are strange as can be. Different things are valued here and we have a lot to learn..." (Vogler, 135). In *First Blood,* Teasle and his men hunt Rambo like a wild animal. Originally wanting nothing more than a bite to eat, Rambo must now fight for his life. For a good part of the journey afterward, he faces a number of challenges during which all of his skills as a Green Beret are utilized as he successfully neutralizes all of the men hunting him. Terrified, they retreat, but plan to return with bigger, stronger reinforcements. At this point in the journey, heroes will meet a "mentor" of some kind, a friend, magician or helper and John Rambo is no different. Colonel Sam Trautman, the man who trained Rambo in Vietnam arrives on scene.

He tries to convince him to surrender, but Rambo refuses. The Descent culminates with entrance into "the innermost cave," the mid-point to Act Two and the beginning of the hero's Initiation where he faces "all the final preparations for the Supreme Ordeal. It often brings heroes to a stronghold of the opposition, a defended center where every lesson… of the journey so far comes into play. New perceptions are put to the test and the final obstacles to reaching the heart are overcome, so that the Supreme Ordeal may begin" (Vogler, 152).

The innermost cave moment usually is associated with a "death and rebirth" of the hero physically, emotionally or spiritually. In *First Blood* the innermost cave is literally a cave. The Soldiers force Rambo into a mine where he becomes trapped when Soldiers blow up the opening, sealing him inside.

The Descent in *First Blood:Part 2* takes place as Rambo and Trautman arrive in Asia at a special CIA outpost. Led by Marshall Murdock, they plan a mission to find evidence of POW's and take photographic evidence. As Rambo begins his mission, another hint at the bigger separation that he has with society appears.

MURDOCK

Colonel, are you sure he's not still unbalanced from the war? We can't afford to have anyone involved who might crack under pressure in that hell.

TRAUTMAN

Pressure? Let me just say that Rambo's the best combat Vet I've ever seen. A pure fighting machine with only a desire, to win a war someone else lost, and if winning means he has to die, he'll die. No fear. No regrets... one more thing... what you choose to call "Hell", he calls home. (Stallone/Cameron, 11. Emphasis added)

As with all great journeys, the Descent is full of enemies, tests and allies. Rambo makes an ally with a Vietnamese woman name Co, who leads him to the prison camp. Supposedly abandoned and empty, Rambo discovers a dozen American prisoners. Rather than take photos, he rescues one and heads towards the extraction point with the Vietnamese army in full pursuit. As he and the prisoner make it to the extraction point, Murdock aborts the mission with the helicopter only feet from landing. Rambo's allies become his enemy and their betrayal marks his Approach to the Innermost Cave.

In *Rambo III*, Rambo "descends" to the deserts of Afghanistan where he, as always, faces enemies, tests and allies. The allies appear in the form of Afghani freedom fighters; the enemies in the form of the Russian forces that have come to occupy them. Here, Rambo approaches the "inner most cave" when he sneaks into the prison that holds Trautman. When the rescue goes awry, he descends even further by escaping through an underground sewer system. In *Rambo,* the allies come in the form of a team of mercenaries who initially reject Rambo altogether. Later, when they overwhelmed by Burmese soldiers, Rambo arrives in time to save them. This part of Rambo's journey shows that he's evolving beyond being just a hero as he takes up the role of the Mentor, puts together a plan and leads the effort to rescue the missionaries.

CHAPTER FIVE

The Initiation

As stated earlier, the "innermost cave" is where the hero faces his toughest challenges thus far; approaching death, but not crossing over. Not the climax of the story, but the crises that marks the mid-point of Act Two.

"The simple secret of the Ordeal is this: **Heroes must die so that they can be reborn...** In some way in every story, heroes face death or something like it: their greatest fears, the failure of an enterprise, the end of a relationship, the death of an old personality, Most of the time the magically survive this death and are literally or symbolically reborn to reap the consequences of having cheated death. They have passed the main test of being a hero" (Vogler, 155).

In *First Blood,* the soldiers declare decisive victory after destroying the cave entrance as they believe that Rambo is dead. For Rambo, it's the start of his Initiation.

> "The way grows dark and narrow. You must go alone on hands and knees and you feel the earth press close around you. You can hardly breathe. Suddenly you come out into the deepest chamber and find yourself face-to-face with a towering figure, menacing Shadow composed of all your doubts and fears... in this moment is the chance to win all or die. No matter what you came for, it's Death that now stares back at you. Whatever the outcome of the battle, you are about to taste death and it will change you" (Campbell, 97).

With no means to escape, Rambo must venture deeper into the mine in an effort to find a way out. The walls narrow, the ceiling lowers, the chambers begin to fill with water... everything closes in on him. When his torch has nearly faded and all seems lost, Rambo finds an exit to the cave. Freedom is his. "With the crises of the Ordeal passed, heroes now experience the consequences of surviving death. With the dragon that dwelt in the Inmost Cave slain or vanquished, they seize the sword of victory and lay claim to their Reward" (Vogler, 175). "You're different. You've changed. Part of you had died and something new has been born. You and the world will never seem the same. This too is part of the Reward for facing death (Campbell, 173). Rambo has escaped certain death.

At this point in *First Blood: Part 2*, Rambo is tortured, beaten and interrogated. With the help of his previous ally Co, he escapes. Once more pursued by the army, he systematically kills most of them off. In *Rambo 3*, the Initiation comes when he re-enters the prison after scaling a cliff and successfully rescues his mentor. Pursued, they eventually find refuge in another cave, where elite special forces soldiers close in on them. Metaphorically, this scene enhances the evolution of Rambo's character. Trautman no longer stands as a mystical force that comes to free Rambo. Rather, this time both the hero and mentor are in harm's way and they are only able to escape by working together. In *Rambo*, everyone in the group experiences the Initiation when an entire battalion of the Burmese Army gives chase. Rambo leads the army away from the group in an attempt to give the missionaries time to escape. He successfully avoids capture, but discovers upon returning to the boat that the rest of the group has not been so lucky.

CHAPTER SIX

The Return

"The Road Back is a turning point, another threshold crossing which marks the passage from Act Two to Act Three. In effect, the Road Back causes the third act. It can be another moment of crises that sets the hero on a new and final road of trials. Often heroes are motivated to hit The Road Back when the forces they have defied in the Ordeal now rally and strike back at them. If the elixir was stolen from the central forces rather than given freely, there may be dangerous repercussions" (Vogler, 189).

In *First Blood*, Rambo seizes an Army truck and heads back into town for a final showdown with the Sheriff. His sights set on retaliation for the injustice he has faced, Rambo blows up a gas station, a gun store and most of the energy grids in town before making his way to the jail where the Sheriff awaits. The climax to Act Three is a short one where Rambo lays waste to the jail and shoots the Sheriff several times. The moment before he kills Teasle, Col. Trautman reappears. He urges Rambo to stop. Vogler calls this moment "the resurrection." "This is the climax, the last and most dangerous meeting with death. Heroes have to undergo a final purging and purification before reentering the Ordinary World. Once more they must change" (Vogler, 197). In the beginning, Rambo was a solitary figure, already an outcast to Teasle's Ordinary World. The confrontation with Trautman reveals the truth: Rambo still carries deep psychological scars from the war, as well as feelings of complete incompetence.

RAMBO

Nothing is over! You don't just turn it off! It wasn't my war! They asked me, I didn't ask them! I killed what I had to kill to win. Come home ready to kiss the ground and see all these maggots at the airport protesting me, spittin'… calling me a baby killer. In the field we had a code of honor. You watch my back, I watch yours. Over here there is nothin'! Over there I could drive tanks, fly gunships, I was in charge of million dollar equipment. Over here, I can't even hold a job parking cars! (Stallone/Giler, 112)

He continues by revealing his deepest scar:

RAMBO

There's blood and pieces of him all over me. I tried to hold him together, but his insides kept slipping through my hands....I still dream about it. I dream about it nearly every night. I wake up and don't know where the fuck I am. I don't talk to anybody for hours, days sometimes. I try to block it out of my mind, but I can't (Ibid).

Rambo breaks down, sobbing into the shoulder of Col. Trautman. While his physical journey has come full circle, Rambo has finally started the journey to repairing his soul. That fracture has kept him isolated since returning home. The journey ends with Trautman escorting him out to an awaiting helicopter, the deeper lesson to the ordeal finally realized. In *First Blood: Part 2,* having successfully survived the Ordeal, he "takes the sword" by capturing an enemy gunship. He returns to the prison camp where he lays waste to the army and rescues all of the prisoners. Rambo and the rescued soldiers flee towards the CIA center, pursued by gunships much larger than their own. In one final, climatic battle they destroy their foe and limp back towards home.

EXT. HANGER - MURDOCK'S POV - TELEPHOTO - DAY

> The image of the burning, mortally wounded Huey seems to waver through the long lens. It looks like a death ship, the Flying Dutchman with a crew of corpses and a demon at the helm, coming in out of the sky (Stallone/Cameron, 81).

Rambo "Returns with the Elixir" when he successfully makes it back to base with all of the rescued soldiers. For the majority of stories, the hero at this point chooses to leave the Special World and return to the Ordinary World that they originally left behind.

> "When the hero-quest has been accomplished, through penetration to the source... the adventurer still must return with his life-transmuting trophy. The full round, the norm of the monomyth, requires that the

hero shall now begin the labor of bringing the runes of wisdom… back into the kingdom of humanity, where the boon may redound to the renewing of the community, the nation, the planet. But the responsibility has been frequently refused" (Campbell, 193).

Here, Stallone and Cameron choose the latter and break with the storytelling convention of the day by having Rambo walk off into the Vietnamese jungle.

TRAUTMAN

You can't keep running. You're free now… Come back with us.

RAMBO

Back to what? -- My friends died here… part of me died here.

TRAUTMAN

How will you live, John?

RAMBO

Day by day.

Rambo walks with his head held high until he fades into the smoke and distance (Stallone/Cameron, 84).

For him, the Special World has become Ordinary. In *Rambo 3*, the Return follows as Rambo and the Mentor race for the Pakistani border. On the verge of freedom, all seems lost when Russian soldiers suddenly surround them. An intense battle follows in which Rambo "takes up the sword" when he assumes control of an enemy tank. He lays waste to enemy forces and kills their commander. After one final appeal by the Afghan fighters for Rambo to stay in this special world, the journey ends with both Rambo and Trautman driving off into the sunset. The Return in *Rambo* happens after the successful rescue. Having healed much of his broken psyche, he returns home to America, finally leaving the special world behind for good.

CHAPTER SEVEN

John Rambo - The 30 Year Journey

Thus far, the Rambo series of films are enhanced when viewed in regard to the individual journey that takes place during each. The character of John Rambo, however, undergoes a journey much bigger than the individual ones of each story, taking over 30 years to complete. "Many stories are about the journey to heal a wound and to restore a missing piece of a broken psyche." (Vogler, 94)

> "Sometimes a hero may seem to be well-adjusted and in control, but that control masks a deep psychic wound. Most of us have some old pain or hurt that we don't think about all the time, but which is always vulnerable on some level of awareness... A hero's wounds and scars mark the areas in which he is guarded, defensive, weak and vulnerable. A hero may

also be extra-strong in some areas as a defense for the wounded parts." (Vogler, 93)

The Separation happens in *First Blood*. Rambo makes his first appearance already fully separated from the "ordinary" world of America. A displaced soldier suffering from post-traumatic stress, psychologically he is no longer able to fit in. Not only does he continue to have recurring nightmares, but the knowledge that he no longer functions normally in the ordinary world weighs heavy.

> "I still dream about it. I dream about it nearly every night. I wake up and don't know where the fuck I am. I don't talk to anybody for hours, days sometimes. I try to block it out of my mind, but I can't. In the field we had a code of honor. You watch my back, I watch yours. Over here there is nothin'! Over there I could drive tanks, fly gunships, I was in charge of million dollar equipment. Over here, I can't even hold a job parking cars!" (Stallone/Giler, 112)

The "call to adventure" comes when police abuse triggers his trauma. He immediately goes into his default "warrior mode" to survive. Most call's to adventure end when the hero has a "meeting with the mentor" who offers advice, special powers or skills or other mystical type help. Here, Col. Trautman comes to the aid of Rambo and convinces him to surrender. The momentary pause initiated by Trautman snaps Rambo out of his warrior mode and results in an emotional breakdown triggered by his memories of the war. A small part of his psyche heals and the true call to adventure – the journey to heal his soul, begins.

The Descent in *First Blood: Part 2* begins with Rambo in prison, which offers an environment of total control and regulation. An environment in which Rambo feels comfortable. This comfort lasts only briefly before he must face crossing the "first threshold" when Trautman reappears and asks Rambo to return to the special world of Vietnam. True healing can only come about from facing the demons, real and personal, head on.

> "Ready or not, we lope out of the village leaving all things familiar behind... It's difficult to pull away from everything you

know but with a deep breath you go on, taking the plunge into the abyss of the unknown. We enter a strange no-man's-land, a world between worlds, a zone of crossing that may be desolate and lonely... But there's no turning back now, we all feel it; the adventure has begun for good or ill." (Campbell)

Rambo must return to the land that traumatized him in the first place. He must be strong enough to find others like himself and help to set them free as well. This part of the journey is called "approaching the innermost cave" because it represents the darkest, most dangerous part of the hero's journey.

Betrayed by his allies, the Vietnamese capture Rambo once more and he again goes through torture and torment. Facing certain death, he escapes with the help of a Vietnamese woman name "Co". When all looks clear, she asks if he will take her with him back to the states. He agrees, they share a moment of tenderness and it looks as if Rambo has taken another step toward healing past internal scars. Fate, however, plays a cruel trick when Vietnamese soldiers surprise and kill Co. Her death galvanizes Rambo's resolve to finish the mission at hand. He succeeds, but the scars of losing Co have cemented Rambo's desire to stay in this special world and he walks off into the Taiwanese jungle.

TRAUTMAN

John... Where are you going?

RAMBO

... I don't know.

TRAUTMAN

You can't keep running. You're free now... Come back with us.

RAMBO

Back to what? -- My friends died here... part of me died here.

TRAUTMAN

John, the war, everything that happened here may have been wrong, but dammit, John, you can't hate your country for it.

RAMBO

Hate? -- I'd die for it.

TRAUTMAN

Then, what is it you want?

RAMBO

What do I want? I want what they want...
(indicates P.O.W.'s)
And what every other guy who came over here and
spilled his guts and gave everything he had wants...
for our country to love us as much as we love it...
That's what I want.

TRAUTMAN

How will you live, John?

RAMBO

Day by day.

Rambo walks with his head held high until he fades into the smoke and distance.

Joseph Campbell makes reference to the hero's journey by comparing the hero to the myths of old. The "ordinary world" is the tribe that the hero must leave, usually on a quest to save it. For Rambo, part of his separation from the Tribe of America comes from their failure to accept him when he returned from the war. Having overcome his innermost cave in Vietnam, he must now face his Initiation in preparation for the Road Back. That Initiation begins when Trautman tracks him down in Thailand. This time, the mentor asks for his help. Rambo refuses and the mentor, fulfilling his job, reveals to Rambo the way home.

TRAUTMAN

When are you going to come full circle? You said that your war is over. Maybe the one out there is, but not the one inside you. I know the reasons you're here John, but it doesn't work that way. You can try, but you can't get away from what you really are.

RAMBO

And what do you think I am?

TRAUTMAN

A full blooded combat soldier.

RAMBO

Not anymore. I don't want it.

TRAUTMAN

That's too bad, because you're stuck with it. We didn't make you this fighting machine, we just chipped away the rough edges. You're always going to be tearing away at yourself until you come to terms with what you are. Until you come full circle.

RAMBO

I guess I'm not ready yet (Stallone/Lettich, 12).

The mentor realizes that Rambo fights an internal battle with himself. He remains bitter over his initial call to the journey of war, at his rejection when he returned. The only way forward comes through acceptance. Rambo blames others and refuses to accept responsibility for the outcome. Ever since Vietnam, he has been on a personal quest for peace. Later, Rambo learns that enemy forces captured Trautman when he proceeded on his own. When a diplomat informs Rambo that no rescue team can be sent, he volunteers to go on his own.

"The hero facing an Ordeal has moved from his center from the ego to the Self, to the more godlike part of himself. There may also be movement from Self to the group as a hero accepts more responsibility than just looking out for himself. A hero risks individual life for the sake of the larger collective life and wins the right to be called hero." (Vogler, 172) Rambo risks everything to rescue his mentor. He succeeds but he still refuses the Road Back. As he stated earlier, "I guess I'm not ready yet." Trautman completes his job as Mentor, having rescued Rambo originally and having given him the words of wisdom that will eventually set him on the path to Return.

"The Road Back marks a time when the heroes rededicate themselves to the adventure. A plateau of comfort has been reached and heroes must be pried off that plateau, either by their own inner resolve or by an external force." (Vogler, 189) *Rambo*, the final film in the overall journey, finds Rambo living a monastic life in Thailand, fully withdrawn from the outside world. It appears that he has settled into a comfortable existence as a recluse.

Far removed from the past experiences of unbelievable violence and force, the peace he has found has not changed his resolve to rejoin the ordinary world. When missionaries arrive asking for his services as a boat ferry, events are set in place to enable Rambo to embrace the Road Back. Originally resistant to helping, the gentle reminders of a woman begin to crack his hard layers of armor.

SARAH

> *Maybe… maybe you lost your faith in people. But you must still be faithful to something. You must still care about something. Maybe we can't change what is. But trying to save a life isn't wasting your life, is it?* (Stallone, 14)

Her statement impacts Rambo at his very core as her question awakens a part of him that he had nearly forgotten. His entire journey, all that he has done in his life in regards to fighting and killing, has been about trying to save the lives of others. Her commitment persuades him to help. She next reminds Rambo of the Ordinary World, something he hasn't thought of for many years.

SARAH

You know, you never told us your name.

RAMBO

John.

SARAH

Where are you from?

RAMBO

Bowie, Arizona.

SARAH

Why'd you leave?

RAMBO

I got drafted into Vietnam.

SARAH

And you just stayed?

RAMBO

It's complicated.

SARAH

You have family back home?

RAMBO

Father, maybe, I don't know.

SARAH

Aren't you curious to see how things might have changed back home? (Stallone, 16)

When enemy forces capture the missionaries and take them prisoner, Rambo takes his final step on his journey. He receives a little supernatural assistance from his old Mentor, Col. Trautman, who visits him in a dream and reminds him that in order to experience full healing, he must come full circle. The Road Back begins when the hero "Seizes the Sword." In this instance, after such a long separation from the ordinary world, Rambo has no sword and must forge his own. Just as it takes heat and pressure to form a strong blade, so too has Rambo's journey metaphorically shaped him into who he is. As he pounds the molten steel into shape, he also pounds out the final traumas of his soul.

Rambo pounds at the red hot steel, forming a large knife blade.

RAMBO (v.o.)

You know what you are. What you're made of. War is in your blood. Don't fight it.

He plunges the steel into a barrel of water, then continues to pound the blade with his hammer.

RAMBO (v.o.)

You didn't kill for your country. You killed for yourself. The gods are never going to make that go away.

Again he plunges the blade into the water.

RAMBO

When you're pushed... killin' is as easy as breathin'.

He holds up the blade that is forming: big, brutal, lethal. (p.35)

Rambo has crossed the final threshold by taking full responsibility for his past. By doing so, he moves on to a new future. After successfully rescuing the missionaries, he finally returns home to America. In the initial introduction to Rambo in *First Blood* he walks along a dreary, lonely road dressed in his old

Army fatigues and carrying his military issue duffle bag. The journey ends with Rambo as he walks along a desolate road in similar fashion.

This time he stops at a mail box that reads R. Rambo and looks towards the small ranch in the distance. He pauses, and looks back down the long, empty highway that he has come from. The road represents the long, lonely journey that he has been through over the past 30 years. He continues towards the farm in the distance finally at peace with his past.

John Rambo has come full circle.

John Rambo has finally come home.

Epilogue

Joseph Campbell was adamant that the Hero's Journey was timeless, that the stages of the journey were contained in all great stories. What Stallone accomplished with the Rambo series in terms of critical and financial success lends strong credence to those theories.

Campbell's work was not widely recognized until the late 1980's, *after* Stallone had written the first three Rambo stories. While Stallone *may have* been aware of Campbell's discourses, it's entirely possible that part of his genius as a writer is that he managed to intuitively tap into this universal mythology before it was widely studied or know.

The journey that John Rambo went through, both individually in each film, and collectively over the entire series, remains a prime example of not only the timelessness of Joseph Campbell's Hero's Journey, but also the Inherent Genius of Sylvester Stallone: Hollywood's Most Underappreciated Writer.

Works Cited

Campbell, Joseph. *The Hero with a Thousand Faces*. Princeton: Princeton University Press, 1968

"Joseph Campbell." 2012. Biography.com 22 Feb 2012, 6:05

http://www.biography.com/people/joseph-campbell-9236309

Stallone, Sylvester and Cameron, James. <u>Rambo: First Blood Part 2</u> *(Screenplay)*

Stallone, Sylvester and Giler, David. <u>First Blood</u> *(Screenplay)*

Stallone, Sylvester and Lettich, Sheldon. <u>Rambo 3</u> *(Screenplay)*

Stallone, Sylvester. <u>Rambo.</u> *(Screenplay)*

Vogler, Christopher. *The Writers Journey: Mythic Structure for Writers*. California: Michael Wiese Productions, 2007.

Printed in Great Britain
by Amazon